Distractible Girl

a guide to the next five minutes of your life

Avril O'Reilly

ISBN: 978-179-581-757-8

DEDICATION

for Distractible girls of all ages

OK

what task am I working on right now?

Any useful info relevant to this task?

where is the WORK stored?

SO

DiD I make PROGRESS?

was I interRUPteD?

what next?
(NEW TaSK OR Start Again)

off I go again

OK

what task am I working on right now?

Any useful info relevant to this task?

where is the work stored?

SO

DiD I make PROGRESS?

was I interRUPteD?

what next?
(NEW TasK OR Start Again)

OK

what task am I working on right now?

Any useful info relevant to this task?

where is the work stored?

SO

DiD I make PROGRESS?

was I interrupted?

what next?
(NEW TaSK OR Start Again)

off I go again

OK

what task am I working on right now?

Any useful info relevant to this task?

where is the work stored?

SO

DiD I make PROGRESS?

was I interrupted?

what next?
(NEW Task OR Start Again)

off I go again

OK

what task am I working on right now?

Any useful info relevant to this task?

where is the work stored?

SO

DiD I make PRogRess?

was I interrupted?

what next?
(New Task or Start Again)

OK

what task am I working on right now?

Any useful info relevant to this task?

where is the WORK STORED?

SO

DiD I make PROgRess?

was I interrupted?

what next?
(NEW Task oR start Again)

off I go again

OK

what task am I working on right now?

Any useful info relevant to this task?

where is the WORK stored?

SO

DiD I make PRogRess?

was I interrupteD?

what next?
(New Task or Start Again)

off I go again

DAY AND DATE..

OK

what task am I working on right now?

Any useful info relevant to this task?

where is the WORK STORED?

SO

DiD I make PRogRess?

was I interRupteD?

what next?
(New Task or start Again)

OK

what task am I working on right now?

Any useful info relevant to this task?

where is the work stored?

SO

DiD I make PROgRESS?

was I interrupteD?

what next?
(NEW TASK OR StARt AGAIN)

off I go again

OK

what task am I working on right now?

Any useful info relevant to this task?

where is the work stored?

SO

DID I make PROGRESS?

was I interrupted?

what next?
(NEW TASK OR start Again)

off I go again

OK

what task am I working on right now?

Any useful info relevant to this task?

where is the work stored?

SO

DiD I make PROGRESS?

was I interRupteD?

what next?
(NEW TASK OR Start Again)

off I go again

DAY AND DATE...

OK

what task am I working on right now?

Any useful info relevant to this task?

where is the work stored?

SO

Did I make progress?

was I interrupted?

what next?
(new task or start again)

OK

what task am I working on right now?

Any useful info relevant to this task?

where is the work stored?

SO

DiD I make PRogRess?

was I interRUpteD?

what next?
(New Task or Start Again)

OK

what task am I working on right now?

Any useful info relevant to this task?

where is the work stored?

SO

DiD I make PRogRess?

was I interRUpteD?

what next?
(NEW Task oR staRt Again)

off I go again

OK

what task am I working on right now?

Any useful info relevant to this task?

where is the work stored?

SO

DiD I make PROGRESS?

was I interrupted?

what next?
(NEW TasK oR staRt Again)

off I go again

OK

what task am I working on right now?

Any useful info relevant to this task?

where is the WORK stored?

SO

DiD I make PRogRess?

was I interrupted?

what next?
(New Task oR start Again)

off I go again

DAY AND DATE..

OK

what task am I working on right now?

Any useful info relevant to this task?

where is the WORK stored?

SO

DiD I make PRoGRESS?

was I interRUpteD?

what next?
(NEW TaSK oR StaRt Again)

OK

what task am I working on right now?

Any useful info relevant to this task?

where is the work stored?

SO

DiD I make PROGRESS?

was I interrupteD?

what next?
(NEW Task OR Start Again)

off I go again

OK

what task am I working on right now?

Any useful info relevant to this task?

where is the work stored?

SO

Did I make Progress?

was I interrupted?

what next?
(New Task or Start Again)

off I go again

OK

what task am I working on right now?

Any useful info relevant to this task?

where is the work stored?

SO

DiD I make PROGRESS?

was I interrupted?

what next?
(NEW TASK OR start Again)

off I go again

OK

what task am I working on right now?

Any useful info relevant to this task?

where is the WORK stored?

SO

Did I make Progress?

was I interrupted?

what next?
(New Task or Start Again)

off I go again

OK

what task am I working on right now?

Any useful info relevant to this task?

where is the work stored?

SO

DiD I make PROGRESS?

was I interrupted?

what next?
(NEW TASK OR start Again)

off I go again

OK

what task am I working on right now?

Any useful info relevant to this task?

where is the WORK stored?

SO

DiD I make PRoGRess?

was I interRupteD?

what next?
(New Task oR start Again)

off I go again

OK

what task am I working on right now?

Any useful info relevant to this task?

where is the WORK stored?

SO

DiD I make PRogRess?

was I interrupteD?

what next?
(NEW Task OR Start Again)

off I go again

OK

what task am I working on right now?

Any useful info relevant to this task?

where is the work stored?

SO

DiD I make PROGRESS?

was I interrupted?

what next?
(NEW TASK OR START Again)

off I go again

OK

what task am I working on right now?

Any useful info relevant to this task?

where is the WORK stored?

SO

DiD I make PROGRESS?

was I interrupted?

what next?
(NEW TASK OR START Again)

off I go again

OK

what task am I working on right now?

Any useful info relevant to this task?

where is the WORK stored?

SO

DiD I make PROGRESS?

was I interrupted?

what next?
(NEW TaSK OR StaRt Again)

off I go again

OK

what task am I working on right now?

Any useful info relevant to this task?

where is the work stored?

SO

DiD I make PROGRESS?

was I interrupted?

what next?
(NEW TaSK OR StaRt Again)

off I go again

OK

what task am I working on right now?

Any useful info relevant to this task?

where is the work stored?

SO
DiD I make PROGRESS?

was I interRUPteD?

what next?
(NEW Task OR Start Again)

off I go again

OK

what task am I working on right now?

Any useful info relevant to this task?

where is the work stored?

SO

DiD I make PROGRESS?

was I interrupted?

what next?
(NEW TASK OR start Again)

OK

what task am I working on right now?

Any useful info relevant to this task?

where is the work stored?

SO

DiD I make PRogRess?

was I interrupted?

what next?
(New Task or Start Again)

off I go again

OK

what task am I working on right now?

Any useful info relevant to this task?

where is the work stored?

SO

DiD I make PRogRess?

was I interrupted?

what next?
(NEW TasK oR StaRt Again)

off I go again

OK

what task am I working on right now?

Any useful info relevant to this task?

where is the WORK stored?

SO

DiD I make PRogREss?

was I interRUPteD?

what next?
(NEW TaSK OR STArT AGAIN)

off I go again

OK

what task am I working on right now?

Any useful info relevant to this task?

where is the WORK stored?

SO

DiD I make PROGRESS?

was I interrupteD?

what next?
(NEW Task OR Start Again)

OK

what task am I working on right now?

Any useful info relevant to this task?

where is the WORK stored?

SO

DiD I make PROGRESS?

was I interRUPteD?

what next?
(NEW TasK OR Start Again)

off I go again

what task am I working on right now?

Any useful info relevant to this task?

where is the work stored?

SO

DiD I make PRogRess?

was I interrupted?

what next?
(New Task or Start Again)

off I go again

OK

what task am I working on right now?

Any useful info relevant to this task?

where is the work stored?

SO

DiD I make PROgRESS?

was I interRUpteD?

what next?
(NEW Task oR start Again)

ABOUT THE AUTHOR

They say you should write the book that you wish existed. Avril O'Reilly is distractible but would like to be focused.
She used her learning about art and her Psychology BA to create this journal to help other distractible girls.

avrilfrances@hotmail.com
avriloreilly.com